WEIGHT-TRAINING

by World Body Building Champion Ralf Möller

WHSMITH
EXCLUSIVE
· BOOKS ·

This edition produced exclusively for
W H Smith

Published in 1990 by
The Hamlyn Publishing Group Limited
Michelin House, 81 Fulham Road, London SW3 6RB

ISBN 0 600 570 533

Produced by Mandarin Offset
Printed and bound in Hong Kong

TABLE OF CONTENTS

FOREWORD

Weight-training like bodybuilding is an activity all can engage in, regardless of whether, like me, they wish to compete in bodybuilding contests, or whether they simply want to lose excess pounds.

It means being a sculptor of your own body. You shouldn't of course forget, in your concern with your body, that you also have a head. It is not indicative of any higher intelligence in people to regard weight-training as an activity for morons. Strangely enough, other sportsmen are not subjected to such prejudice.

Learn about weight-training properly. Like all my colleagues in bodybuilding, I am involved in it heart and soul. Like any other athletic activity, it can do a lot for you: giving you the inner strength, for example, that allows you to take the knocks of life in your stride. In the course of my sporting career, I have come to know many people – people who were there when I needed them. However, I should like to take this opportunity to thank in particular a number of dear friends who helped me on my way through their personal commitment.

These include Walter Herden, with whom I have been friends for years, and Jürgen Brandt with whom I have trained for a number of years and who has made a considerable contribution to my success. Albert Busek set me on the right road at the beginning, and has since done a great deal for me. His wife Gabi, who is fighting a serious illness, has nonetheless always found the strength to encourage other people – including myself. Also my fiancée, Annette, with whom I can always discuss my problems, and last but not least my parents without whom I would have been unable to follow my chosen path and to whom I should therefore like to dedicate this book. I hope that it may help you a little to achieve your sporting objectives, and I wish you success in your sport, and fun in reading about it.

Ralf Möller.

ANATOMY

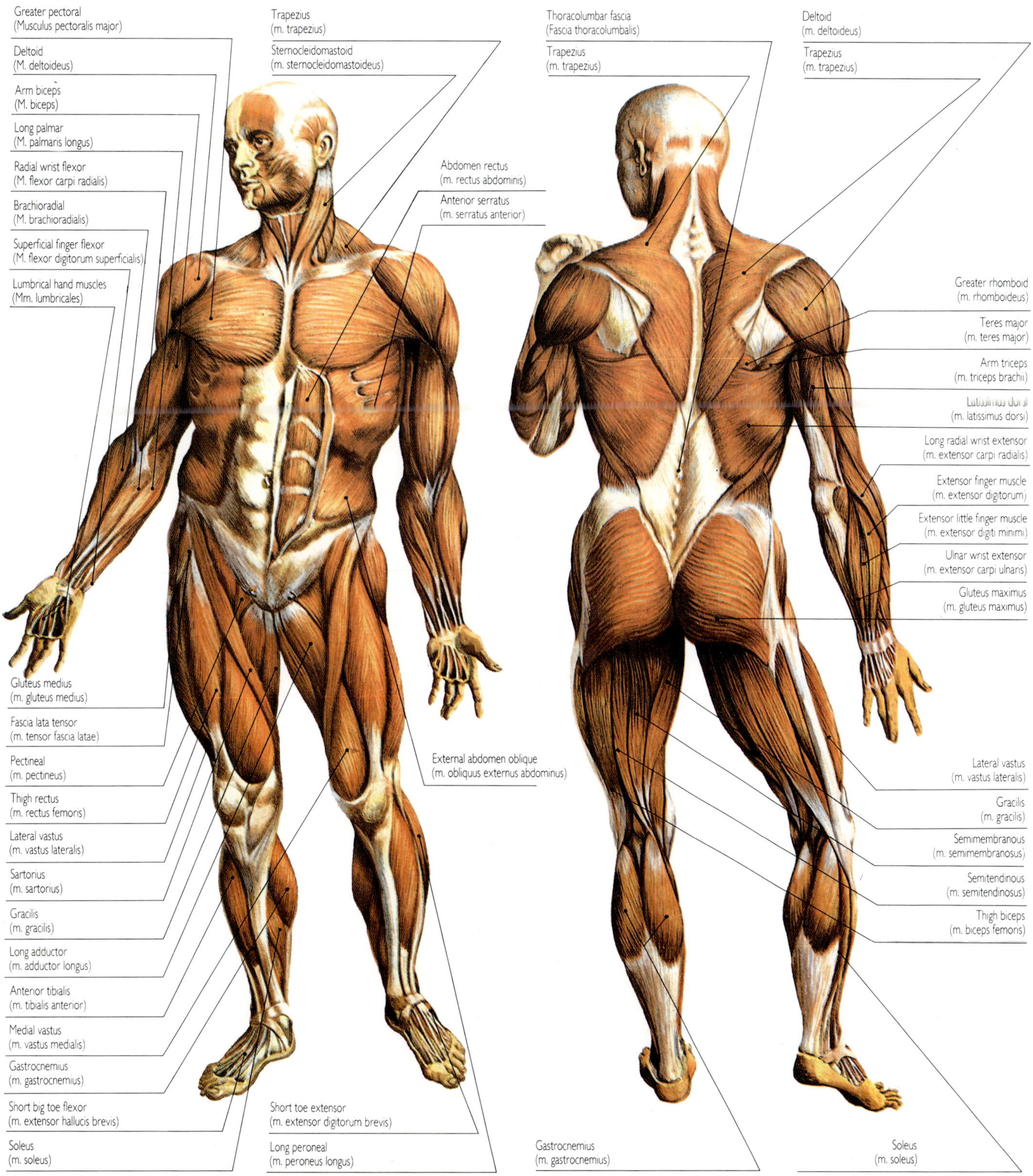
Greater pectoral
(Musculus pectoralis major)
Deltoid
(M. deltoideus)
Arm biceps
(M. biceps)
Long palmar
(M. palmaris longus)
Radial wrist flexor
(M. flexor carpi radialis)
Brachioradial
(M. brachioradialis)
Superficial finger flexor
(M. flexor digitorum superficialis)
Lumbrical hand muscles
(Mm. lumbricales)
Gluteus medius
(m. gluteus medius)
Fascia lata tensor
(m. tensor fascia latae)
Pectineal
(m. pectineus)
Thigh rectus
(m. rectus femoris)
Lateral vastus
(m. vastus lateralis)
Sartorius
(m. sartorius)
Gracilis
(m. gracilis)
Long adductor
(m. adductor longus)
Anterior tibialis
(m. tibialis anterior)
Medial vastus
(m. vastus medialis)
Gastrocnemius
(m. gastrocnemius)
Short big toe flexor
(m. extensor hallucis brevis)
Soleus
(m. soleus)
Trapezius
(m. trapezius)
Sternocleidomastoid
(m. sternocleidomastoideus)
Abdomen rectus
(m. rectus abdominis)
Anterior serratus
(m. serratus anterior)
External abdomen oblique
(m. obliquus externus abdominus)
Short toe extensor
(m. extensor digitorum brevis)
Long peroneal
(m. peroneus longus)
Thoracolumbar fascia
(Fascia thoracolumbalis)
Trapezius
(m. trapezius)
Gastrocnemius
(m. gastrocnemius)
Deltoid
(m. deltoideus)
Trapezius
(m. trapezius)
Greater rhomboid
(m. rhomboideus)
Teres major
(m. teres major)
Arm triceps
(m. triceps brachii)
(m. latissimus dorsi)
Long radial wrist extensor
(m. extensor carpi radialis)
Extensor finger muscle
(m. extensor digitorum)
Extensor little finger muscle
(m. extensor digiti minimi)
Ulnar wrist extensor
(m. extensor carpi ulnaris)
Gluteus maximus
(m. gluteus maximus)
Lateral vastus
(m. vastus lateralis)
Gracilis
(m. gracilis)
Semimembranous
(m. semimembranosus)
Semitendinous
(m. semitendinosus)
Thigh biceps
(m. biceps femoris)
Soleus
(m. soleus)

THE CHEST

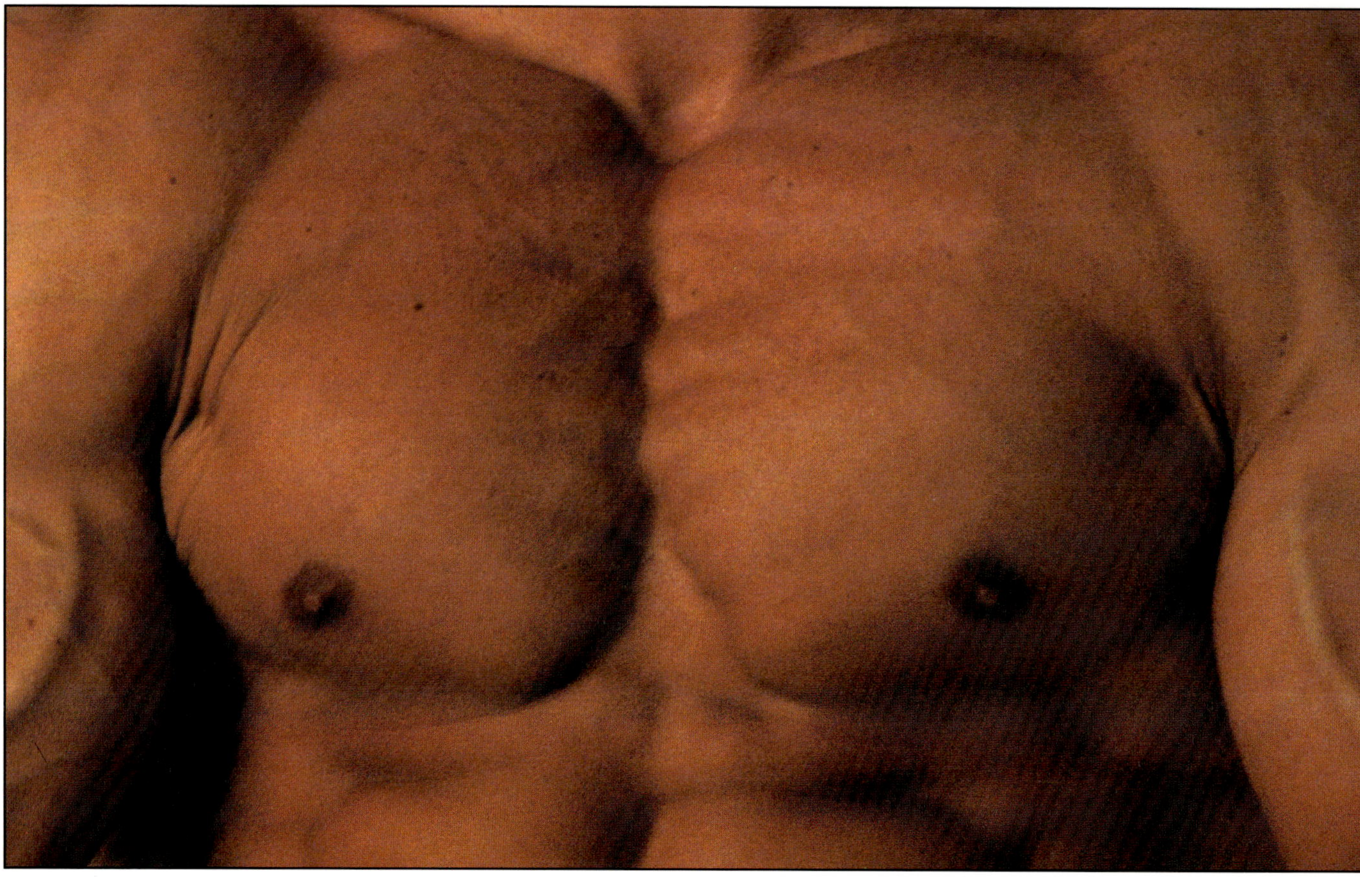

TRAINING AND EXERCISE

The chest muscles undoubtedly form one of the main groups of muscles. Competitive athletes, in particular, have to train this set of muscles continuously with various exercises. Given my size and broad chest, I initially found it particularly difficult to develop the right muscles mass in this area. So one of the most important exercises for the upper and lower chest area for me was the bench presss, where my best performance at a later stage was 529lb. If you consider the leverage difficulties I have due to my body size, then you will realize what it means to press this weight. In chest training you should never forget that you are also training some of the shoulder muscles, and also the triceps. For this reason, one of my four programmes, for example, involves training the biceps after the main muscle group of the chest, as they have so far not been exercised. For the upper area of the chest muscles, I recommend the incline bench press with barbells or dumbbells. The Multipress is also excellent for this muscle area. For separation of the chest muscles there is no better exercise than the flying exercise with dumbbells. You can complete the programme with pull-overs, working either with barbells or with dumbbells. Make sure when doing the pull-overs that your head is on the bench, as this exerts particular stress on the inner and upper parts of the chest. Four weeks before contests, I then build two-armed cable rows into the programme.

BARBELL BENCH PRESS

The barbell bench press is an excellent exercise for muscle mass. Grip the bar with the hands slightly more than shoulder width apart. Breathe in as you lower the barbell. The bar must touch the chest. Breathe out as you press outwards. You can also do this exercise repeatedly on the multi-purpose tower. It is very good for beginners as they can get into the sequence of the exercise better with the aid of the chest machine. We are also exercising the shoulders and triceps here.

FREE DUMBBELL BENCH PRESSES

The sequence of movements in the dumbbell press is similar to that in the barbell exercise, but puts less strain on the shoulders, and you have a greater radius of movement on lowering. Here again: breathe in as you lower, breathe out as you raise.

INCLINE DUMBBELL FLYES

Here we have an exercise for dividing the chest muscles in the outer and inner area. The arms and legs are slightly bent. When lowering the arms, the head rises slightly and the thighs move slightly towards the head. Once again: breathe in on lowering, breathe out on raising.

MY TIP

Before choosing a fitness training centre, you should go through a trial training session. The important factors are atmosphere, assistance from trained specialist staff, and a variety of training facilities.

PULLEY ROWS

The pulley row is an exercise designed solely to train muscle definition. I incorporate it in my training for the last few weeks before a contest. It is important to stand firm and solid. The back must be straight with the upper body bent slightly forward. The arms are slightly bent. When pulling together, breathe out, and when moving the arms apart, breathe in. The legs can be slightly bent.

INCLINE BENCH PRESSES ON MÖLLER'S MULTI-PRESS

This is an exercise for the upper part of the chest. It is similar in sequence to the free incline bench presses with the barbells. The advantage of the apparatus is that as well as this exercise, a further 11 can be done on it: bench presses for the chest, presses for the front and rear shoulder muscle, bent over barbell rowing, front and rear squats, calf exercise, lunge, narrow triceps presses, biceps training and lower arm training.

INCLINE BARBELL PRESSES ON THE MULTIPRESS

This exercise, too, is excellent for training the upper chest muscles (Pectoralis minor). I advise beginners to use the Multipress, as the exercise sequence is assisted by the machine. Once again: breathe in as you lower and out as you raise.

DUMBBELL PULL-OVERS

The Dumbbell pull-over is excellent for expanding the rib cage and strengthening the inner chest muscles. The arms are slightly bent. The head should not hang down but should rest on the bench to prevent the exercise from becoming a back exercise. Breathe in on lowering and out on the upward movement.

PECK DECKS

This exercise is extremely good for seperating and striating the chest muscles. Breathe in on stretching, and out on contracting. A good exercise for beginners, as the sequence is dictated by the machine, and it is impossible, therefore, to get it wrong.

DIPS

Dips are a good exercise after chest training, as they put stress on the chest muscles as a whole. They even stress the outer area of the muscles of the lower chest. Breathing: breathe in at the top and out at completion of the movement.

MY TIP

For a bodybuilder intending to take part in contests, it is important to find a partner in whom the muscle groups where you are weak are better trained.

INCLINE BENCH PRESSES

This is an exercise for the upper chest muscles. Grip the bar with the hands slightly more than shoulder width apart. The bench should be at an angle of 40 degrees to avoid putting excessive strain on the shoulders. For proper breathing, breathe in on lowering, out on raising. You can also do this exercise with dumbbells with the same sequence of movements. But here you have more freedom of movement and the chest muscles are expanded more. The dumbbell position should be horizontal.

THE BACK

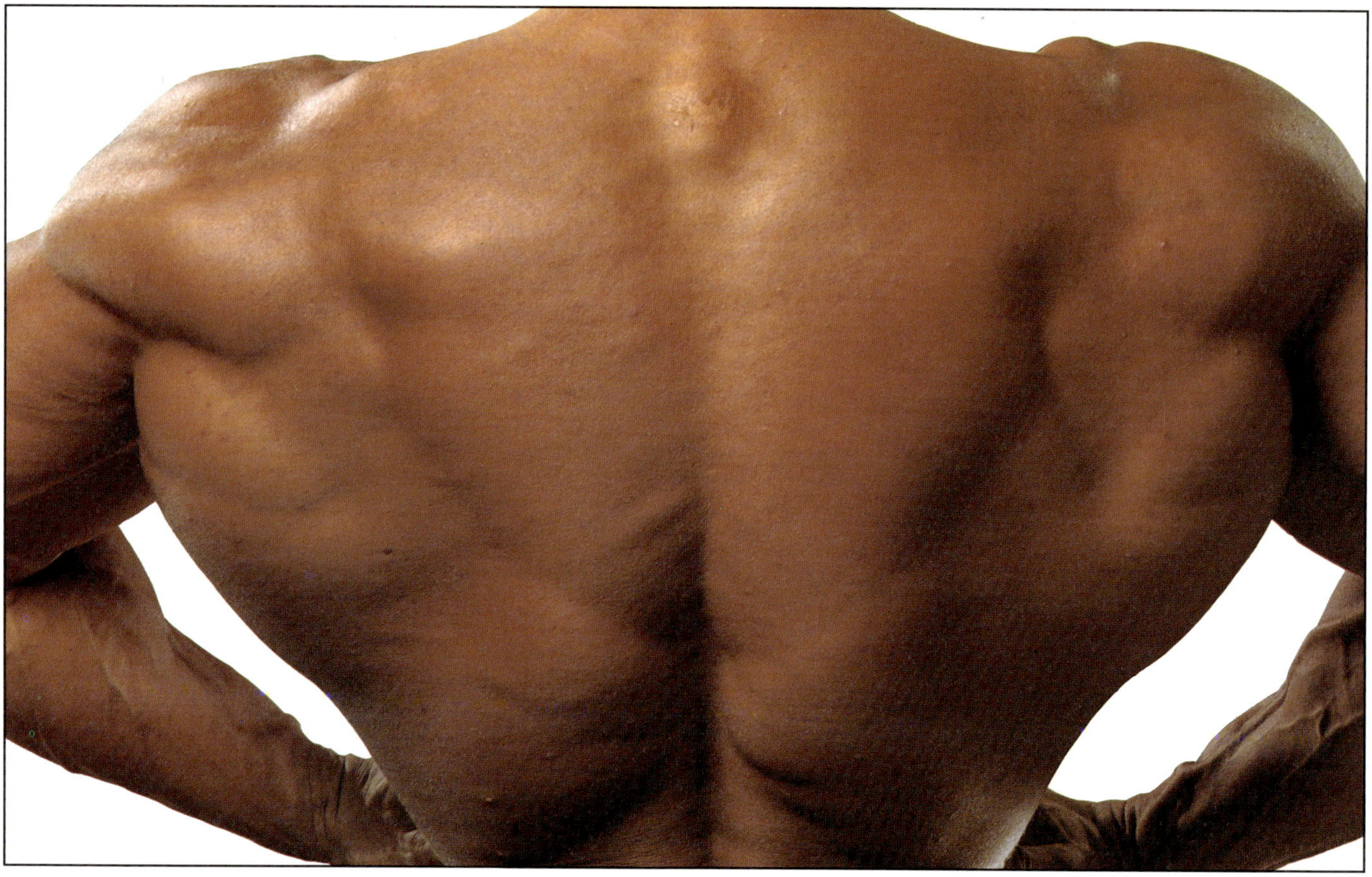

TRAINING EXERCISES

Together with the chest and leg, the back constitutes one of the main groups of muscles. It is therefore important, particularly for competitors, to train dense back muscles, as this can often be the determining factor in success or failure. Before beginning back training, it is very important to know whether you want to improve the width (breadth) of the back, or the mass of the inner area. In all exercises with a wide grip, you put only the inner part under stress; in exercises with a narrow grip, the outer area is stressed. One exercise that I always incorporate into my training programme is the dumbbell row. Here, you bend the upper body forward slightly and, depending on the side you are training, support yourself with the other arm. To increase the stress on the outer back muscle area, you should bend the knees slightly. You should ensure that you pull the dumbbells past as close as possible to the body. I work with dumbbells a lot, particularly for the inner muscles, as I reach the innermost set of muscles in pulling in the dumbbells. For mass building I recommend chin-ups and bent-over barbell rows. One of the main groups of muscles is the tensors of the back, but unfortunately all too often these are assigned inadequate importance as they are not visible at first glance. In most exercises they have to withstand extreme stresses – e.g. in the squat, or in biceps training in the standing position. As many of these exercises distort, the stress is further increased. I advise beginners to train these muscles on the hyperextension bench and later by cross lifting.

CHINS TO FRONT

Here we have an exercise for strengthening the back muscles, particularly the inner area. The hands grip the bar slightly more than shoulder width apart. Breathe in as you raise and out as you lower. The legs should be bent and crossed. The chin should be stretched over the bar so that the upper muscles of the chest touch the bar.

MY TIP

Never eat less than an hour before training. Otherwise you will soon tire and lose motivation.

CHINS TO BACK

For this exercise, the sequence is the same as in the chin-ups, with the difference being that the chin touches the top of the chest and the neck touches the bar on raising.

BENT OVER BARBELL ROWS

There is another exercise for strengthening the back muscles in the inner area. The upper body is bent forwards, and the bar is brought to stomach level on lifting. The legs are slightly bent. The head must be pointing upwards. Breathe in as you raise the barbell, out as you lower it.

MY TIP

You should always wear a weightlifting belt when training 'freestanding', with relatively heavy weights.

DUMBBELL ROWS

The dumbbell row is an exercise for the width of the back, hence for the outer part of the back. To give a better hold, you should take up your position to the side of the bench. Support yourself with one hand on the bench. The knees should be slightly bent, the back straight, with the head pointing upwards. With the free hand, grip the dumbbell and lift it past the body upwards to the side. Once again it is important to breathe correctly: breathe in as you raise, out as you lower.

SEATED PULLEY ROWS: NARROW GRIP

This is an exercise for increasing back width. The upper body is bent forwards, the arms stretched, breathing out. As you straighten the upper body, breathe in, bend the arms in towards the body and bring the grips back at around stomach height. The back should be properly straightened. You can also do this exercise with a wide grip. It then acts on the inner area of the muscles of the lower back. Use a wide grip of approximately shoulder width.

MY TIP

Joint counting of individual repeats in exercises motivates your partner in training, and encourages him to achieve higher performance levels.

SEATED PULLEYS

This is a preliminary exercise for chin-ups. Once again it strengthens the inner area of the back muscles. The posture is straight. As you pull in the weight you breathe in, and as you lower it you breathe out. The cable can be pulled down either behind the head or forwards to the chest.

BENT OVER LATERALS

This back exercise trains the individual muscle heads in the back to even greater definition. When lowering the arms, the upper body is bent forwards, the back straightened, the head raised. The bent arms are then moved upwards, the head moving down and the chin touching the top of the chest. Breathe out with the arms hanging down, and in when the arms are bent upwards. This same exercise can also be carried out seated. Sit only half on the bench (to give greater freedom of movement for the legs). The upper body rests on the legs, the head points upwards. The bent arms point upwards, the hands turning the dumbbells outwards (thumbs downwards).

BENT OVER LATERALS WITH CABLES

This is an exercise for definition of the back muscles in the inner area. The legs are slightly bent, the upper body bent forwards with the back tightened, and the head held up. Move your slightly bent arms up and down. Pay attention to your breathing: breathe in as you raise the arms, and out as you lower them.

HYPER EXTENSIONS

This exercise, too, is good for strengthening the lumbars of the back. The upper body hangs downwards. Before straightening up, place the hands on the back of the neck and lift the head. Rules for breathing: breathe in as you straighten up, out as you complete the movement.

MY TIP

Breathing is an essential part of training. Basically you can assume that you breathe out in each case during the press or pull motion. As you return the weight to the starting position, you breathe in. Never hold your breath during an exercise. This deprives the body of the necessary oxygen and your blood pressure can rise to a dangerous level.

GYM 80
20 KG

T-BAR ROWS

This is an extremely effective exercise for muscle mass and width of back. Here, we adopt a position as if we were about to perform a starting dive. This means that the legs are slightly bent, the small of the back is flattened and the head raised. As you life, you should bend the head forwards. The elbows should be kept as close as possible to the body. Don't forget to breathe correctly: breathe in as you lift the weight, and out as you lower it. T-bar rows on the incline bench are similar to the exercise described above. But here we are putting the inner back area under stress, varying the grip position.

DEADLIFT

The deadlift helps to strengthen the tensors of the back. Grip the barbell with the hands slightly more than shoulder width apart, the left palm facing inwards and the right facing outwards. The legs should be slightly bent, the small of the back flattened and the head facing upwards. The arms remain well stretched and the upper body upright. Breathe in as you straighten the upper body, and out as you bend forward.

ALEX
FITNESS - BODY - LINE
PUMA
ALEX

THE LEGS

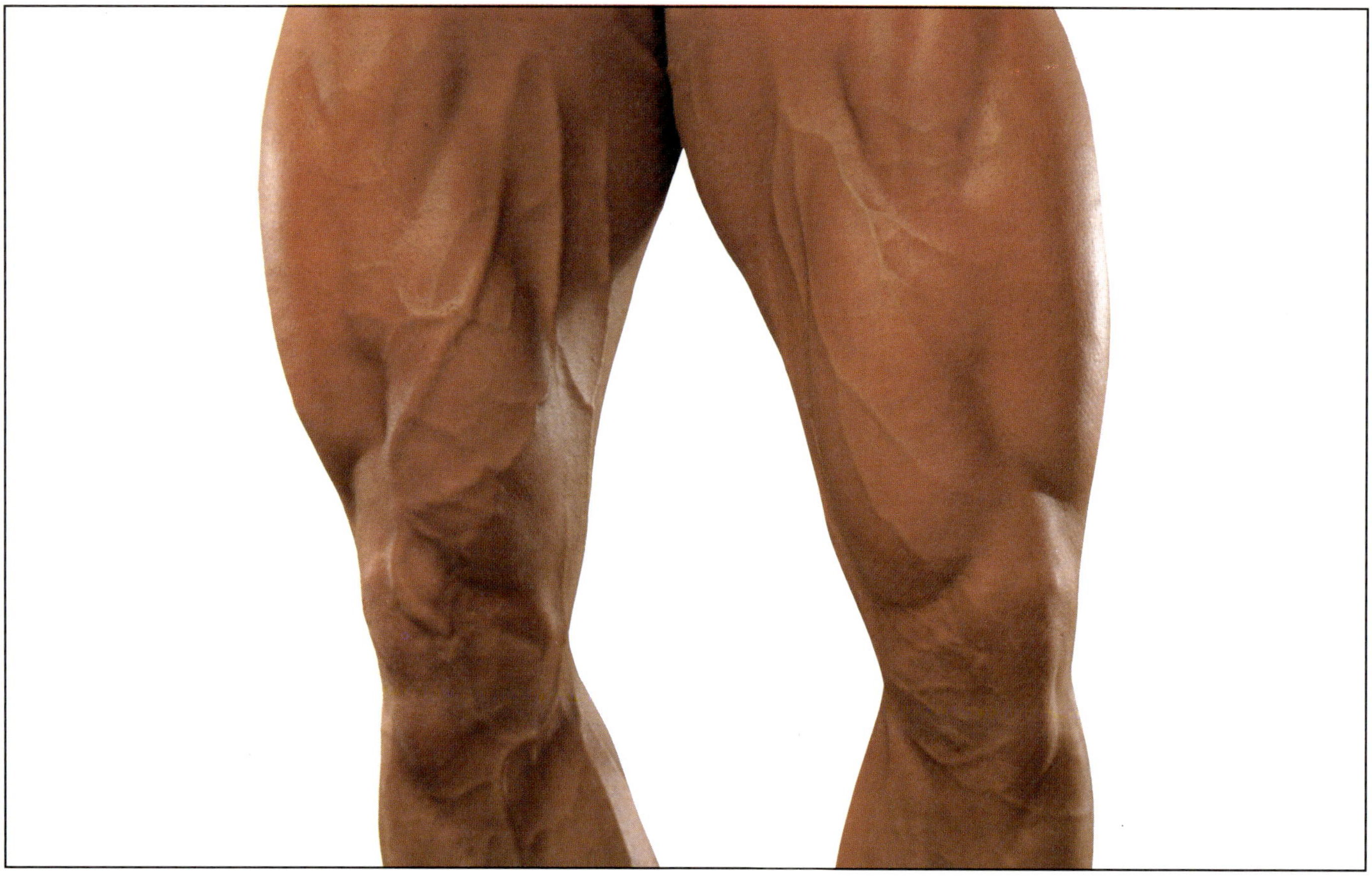

TRAINING EXERCISES

Like the chest and back, the legs have a large proportion of the total muscles of the body. Competitors in particular, for whom harmony plays an important role, should train their legs with as many exercises as possible. The legs should not only be round and thick, but also exhibit form and muscle definition. Beginners in particular tend to neglect this group of muscles, believing the chest and arms to be more important for their appearance. Tall people have particular difficulty in training the legs. It takes considerably longer for them to achieve visible success. With my size, I can speak from experience: it really is very difficult to train muscle mass in this area. The most important exercise is the squat, and this is an exercise in which many mistakes are made. Since the heart and circulation are put under particular stress, you must ensure an adequate supply of oxygen (by opening a window, for example). When doing the exercise, you must ensure that the head is held high so that the back can be kept straight. If you have developed a massive, well defined set of leg muscles to match your upper body, you will find yourself among the finalists in a contest.

BACK SQUATS

The barbell squat is an important exercise for muscle mass on the thighs. it also supports the heart and circulation, whilst at the same time placing this system under the extreme stress. Do make sure that your legs are shoulder width apart with the feet pointing slightly outwards. As you go down, keep the back straight and breathe in. As you come up, breathe out. This exercise also strengthens the bottom.

In contrast to the 'back squat', in the 'front squat' make sure to cross the arms to hold the barbell better. Beginners should place a two to three centimetre slab of wood or barbell disc under the heels to prevent them from losing their balance as they go down.

MY TIP

Lively music can help to achieve a much more harmonious training sequence.

INCLINE LEG PRESSES

This exercise serves to train both the hamstrings and the inside of the thighs which are also called the adductors. The feet should point slightly outwards. The thighs should just touch the upper body. Breathe in on lowering and out when pushing up. As the incline leg press, this exercise is designed exclusively for the hamstrings. Here too, the feet are turned slightly outwards. If possible, the thighs should just touch the body on lowering.

LEG EXTENSIONS

This is an exercise for definition (muscle sharpness). Breathe in on lowering and out on stretching. The feet can be turned alternately inwards and outwards to isolate the individual muscles better.

MY TIP

The knee bend and leg press lead in particular to strained breathing, and therefore to a rise in blood pressure. Those at risk from high blood pressure should thus avoid the highest weights in this instance, and at the first trace of dizziness should incorporate different exercises into their programme. Beginners should ensure that there is sufficient fresh air when carrying out squats as this exercise places extreme stress on the heart and circulation.

Following a stressful day at the office, however, an evening training session generally has a very positive effect on general well-being and gets the circulation going again.

LUNGE

This exercise is particularly good for women, as it trains not only the thighs but also the bottom. Stand as if about to take a large step forward. Then bend at the knees, breathe in, pull up the leg and breathe out. This exercise should be repeated alternately on the left and right legs.

MY TIP

The trained muscle can be placed under new stress by altering the width of the stance.

HACK SQUATS

This exercise is good for the entire quadruceps region especially the area around the knee. Once again, pay attention to your breathing: breathe in as you go down and out as you rise. Remember to keep the back as straight as possible.

LYING LEG CURLS

This curl is specifically designed to train the hamstrings. Breathing: breathe in as you curl, out as you lower. The head should be raised to achieve a better result from the exercise.

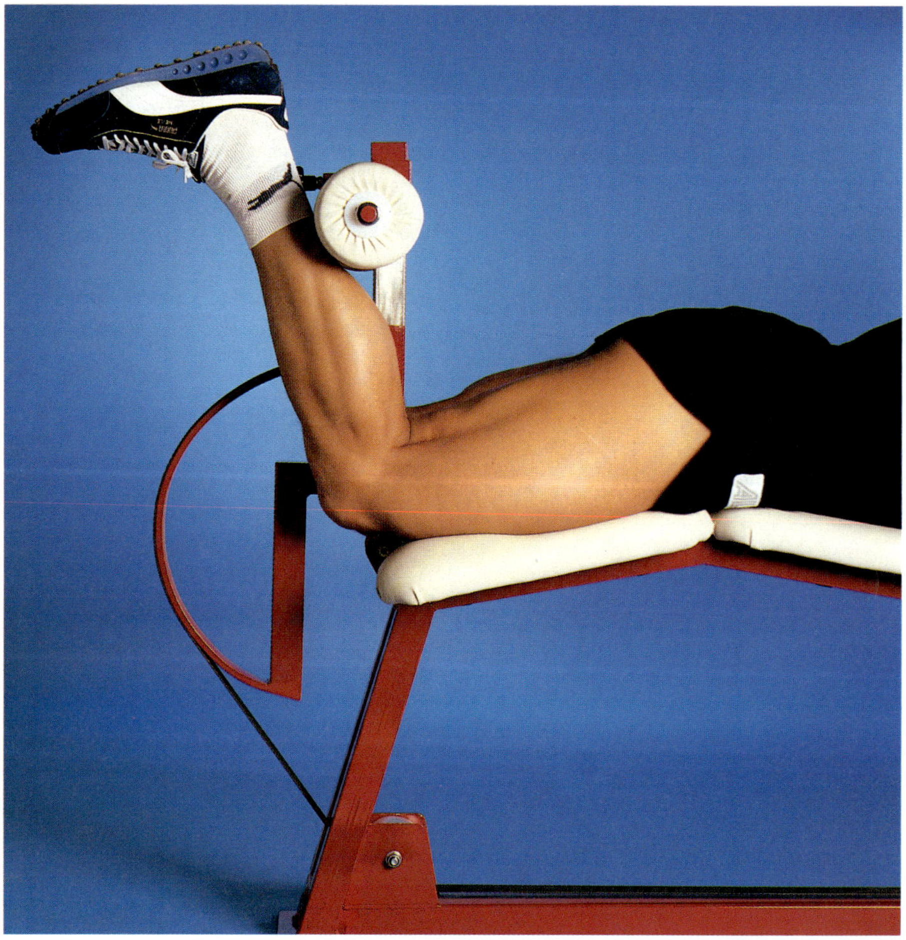

STANDING LEG CURLS

This exercise is based on the same sequence as the lying leg curl, although I find that the hamstring is put under even greater stress in the standing version.

SEATED CALF RAISES

This again is an exercise to improve the definition of the calf muscles. I turn the foot inwards or outwards to train all the muscles correctly.

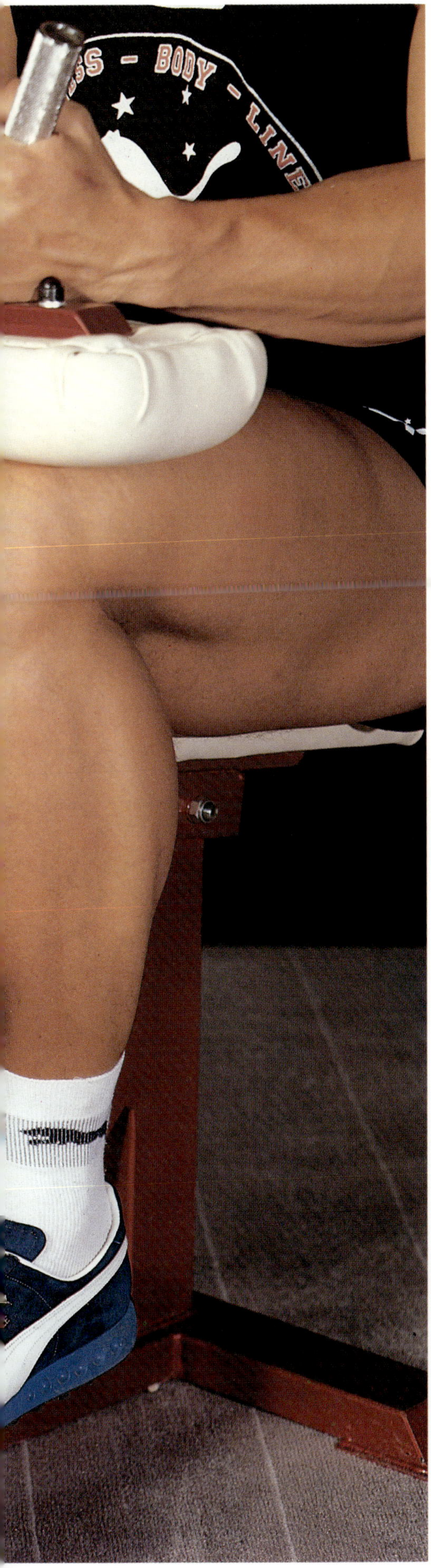

MY TIP

Approximately two hours before training, you should eat more carbohydrate than protein.

DONKEY RAISES

This is an exercise that you can do even without any apparatus. All you need is one or two training partners to sit on your back. The sequence is the same as in the other calf exercises. It is important for the calves to be stretched to the full and the angle of the ball of the foot to be changed relatively frequently so that the large toe points alternately inwards and outwards. My partner in the illustration is Alfred Neugebauer from Vienna who has been taking part in contests for years, and is one of the world's top athletes. In Tokyo, he took fourth place.

STANDING CALF RAISES

This exercise serves to build up calf muscle mass. The sequence is the same as the seated calf raise. Stand with the balls of the feet on the step of the machine, with the heels pointing downwards in the stretched state. When pushing up it is extremely important for the legs to remain straight.

THE ARMS

TRAINING EXERCISES

For many people, the arm muscles are a symbol of strength. For this reason there is also a tendency to train these muscles over frequently and to forget the total harmony of the body. All too often, I find that excessivly heavy weights are used in arm training, following the motto 'More iron, more muscles'. By so doing, the exercise is generally so distorted that the desired effect is almost entirely lost. You should never forget that the biceps is a small muscle that cannot be trained in the same way as the chest and legs. You should therefore do the exercises as correctly as possible. Since the arms are also trained in many exercises, it is sufficient when training three to four times per week for the arms to be put under specific stress only once. To achieve muscle mass in the upper arm, I recommend the standing barbell curl for the biceps and lying narrow triceps presses with the barbell. To give the arm the required shape, you should work with dumbbells. You should also do special lower arm training in the form of the wrist curl with the barbell or dumbbells approximately every 14 days. Apart from this the lower arm is placed under sufficient stress in general arm training.

NARROW BENCH

This exercise is designed to build up triceps mass. The hands should be approximately 15 centimetres apart. Breathe in as you lower and out as you raise.

STANDING TRICEPS PRESSES

This is an exercise designed to build up triceps mass. The upper arms are held against the upper body, with only the lower arms moving up and down.

Bent over triceps exercise at the rope

This is an exercise for triceps muscle definition. It is important to adopt the correct stance and to keep your balance. Breathing rules: breathe in as you bend over, out as you stretch.

FRENCH PRESS

This exercise can be done with a barbell. The head should be leaned slightly backwards. The arms are bent, only the lower arm moving up and down. Once again: breathe in as you lower, out as you stretch. This exercise can also be done with an EZ barbell, which alleviates stress on the joints.

MY TIP

You should always keep up to date by reading good specialist books.

SINGLE ARM TRICEPS EXTENSIONS

This is an exercise both for mass building and muscle definition. It is important to keep the back straight. Once again, only the lower arm moves. The upper arm is placed against the head. The wrist must be kept stiff. Breathe in on lowering and out as you press out.

MY TIP

If you don't understand an exercise, don't be afraid to ask the instructor to explain.

STANDING BARBELL CURLS

This is a mass exercise for the biceps. The upper arms lie against the body, with only the lower arms moving up and down. Correct breathing: breathe in as you curl, out as you lower. Try to perform this exercise as correctly as possible: do not work too much with the upper body.

STANDING DUMBBELL CURLS

The standing dumbbell curl is an exercise for muscle definition and the height of the biceps. Make sure when curling the dumbbells that the little finger is pointing upwards, i.e. turn the hand slightly. Supinate the wrists around so that the palm of the hand is facing the chin. This places excess stress on the biceps.

SEATED DUMBBELL CURLS

The sequence of this exercise is the same as in the standing dumbbell curl. When seated, however, you can concentrate better on the sequence. With added concentration you gain more contraction.

MY TIP

Choose your training wear so that you can observe the muscles being trained and can therefore keep a better check on the exercise.

ALEX
FITNESS - BODY - LINE
PUMA
ALEX

DUMBBELL OR BARBELL CURLS ON THE SCOTT BENCH

This is an exercise which lengthens the head of the biceps. Correct breathing: breathe out as you lower, and in as you curl. Here again, the wrists should be kept as straight as possible. Hang comfortably with your shoulders on the bench as this will enable you to gain peak contraction.

The dumbbell exercise works in particular on definition of the height of the biceps. You should keep the muscles tensed for two to three seconds at the top, and turn the hands inwards to strengthen the contraction.

Both exercises also train the lower arms.

MY TIP

You should sometimes grip the barbell closer together and sometimes further apart, to give the muscle new stimuli. This alternating increases the success of training and you will achieve a greater muscle mass sooner.

30
ALEX

30
ALEX

CONCENTRATION CURLS

The exercise for muscle definition and biceps height is one that I incorporate into my training programme for the last three months before a contest. The arm is initially outstretched, with the upper arm touching the thigh. Only the lower arm moves up and down. The wrist is held straight. Breathing: breathe out as you lower and in as you perform the positive part of the repetition. This exercise can also be performed with an arm curl machine. To achieve a higher intensity and to give biceps definition, you can begin with a relatively high weight, whilst a partner helps you lower the weight.

ALEX

FOREARM TRAINING

This exercise is used to strengthen the lower arm. The thumbs are placed around the barbell, the upper arms are held against the body, and the lower arms move upwards as you breathe in. The palms of the hands point outwards as you curl. Breathe out as you lower the barbell.

BENCH LOWER ARM TRAINING

As an alternative to the previous exercise, take a barbell, but place the lower arm on the knee so that the wrist can move freely, just moving the hands up and down.

MY TIP

For performance-oriented bodybuilding, it is important to find a centre where other competitors also train. Training is much better in company.

THE SHOULDERS

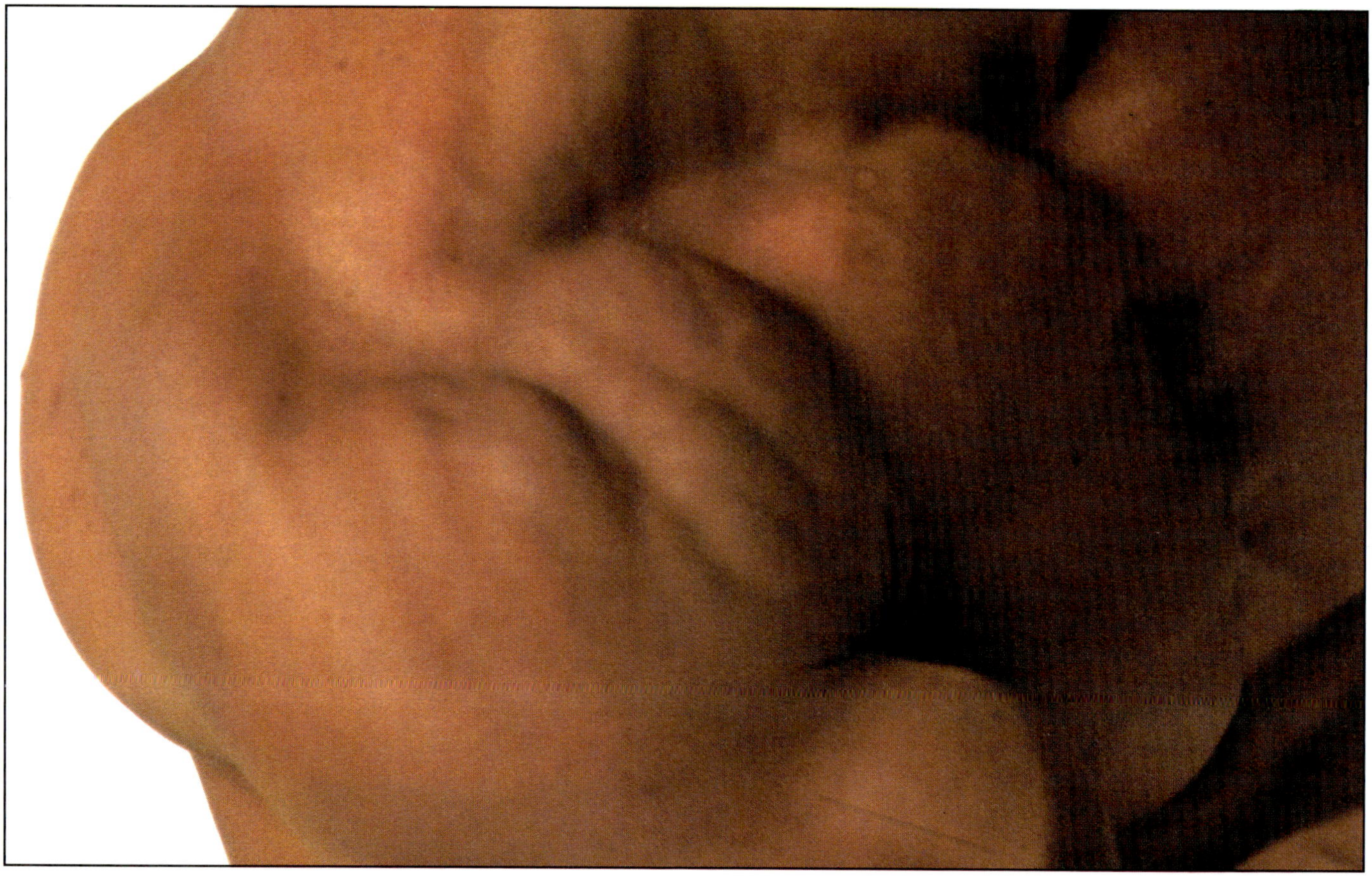

TRAINING EXERCISES

You will doubtless be familiar with the expression 'hulk'. Few people realise that the shoulders play the main part. To get muscle mass on the shoulders, you should work with barbells: I am thinking here of neck and front presses. To strengthen the neck muscle, I recommend upright rowing. The neck is also put under stress in the press exercises. Since the shoulder area is very susceptible to injury – I am also thinking of the bench press here – it is very important to warm up these parts of the body with two sets of exercises. The number of repeats may be around 20. Contest athletes who have wide hips by nature can create the image of a small waist by having wide shoulders.

PRESSES BEHIND THE NECK

This is an exercise to strengthen the muscles of the shoulders and neck. The hands grip the barbell slightly more than shoulder width apart. When lowering the barbell, it touches the neck lightly, and you breathe in. Breathe out as you raise.

MACHINE PRESSES BEHIND THE NECK

The sequence here is the same as with free presses, but the machine stipulates the sequence of movement.

SEATED DUMBBELL PRESSES

In this exercise, all shoulder muscles are placed under stress. On lowering we breathe in, and on raising we breathe out. Because of the freedom of movement, this exercise is also particularly good for muscle mass.

MY TIP

To keep the heart and circulation performing efficiently, it is good practice to run or cycle once or twice a week.

SEATED LATERAL RAISES

This too is a good exercise for strengthening the shoulder muscles. Here, raise the slightly bent arms, ensuring that the hand is rotated slightly so that the thumb points inwards. This exercise assists definition. On raising the dumbbells, breathe in, and on lowering them, breathe out.

CABLE LATERAL RAISES

This is another exercise to strengthen the shoulder muscles. I do it mainly just before the contest. The arm is slightly bent. Breathe in as you raise the arms and out as you lower them. The cable lateral raise is a very good definition exercise.

MY TIP

The contest bodybuilder should practise intensively his freestyle and tensing in the compulsory poses.

UPRIGHT ROWING, BARBELL

This exercise is designed especially to strengthen the neck muscles (the trapezius). The barbell is drawn up under the chin with the arms bent. Breathe in as you lift. Breathe out as you lower, once again tensing the muscles.

UPRIGHT ROWING, CABLE

This is the same exercise as the upright rows with barbell, but once again with the assistance of apparatus. it is thus particularly good for beginners.

MY TIP

You should take measured doses of protein preparations, mineral drinks and vitamin capsules. This can play a part in assisting success in training.

THE ABDOMEN AND WAIST

TRAINING EXERCISES

Whilst corpulence used to be a symbol of wealth and power, today it is more the active, sports-playing, slim person who gains recognition. Anyone with a pot belly is regarded as immobile and unattractive. For this reason, the abdomen and hips are also popular 'areas of attack' for fitness enthusiasts. It is possible to keep the abdomen under control through special exercises and food that is not too fatty and high in calories in the evening. Cycling and running training are also recommended, which are equally good for the hips and abdomen. A competitor with well defined abdomen muscles always makes a better impression on judges. Of course, you do not achieve a well proportioned body in the hip and abdomen area solely through the exercises designed for the purpose, but in conjunction with general body training which takes into account the abdomen and waist.

Do make sure not to overdo it, either by dieting too strictly or by training with heavy weights or at an excessive level of difficulty. Regular training activity is the secret of success. Remember too that success in training is determined by age. If you are over 30 you will have to be more patient about bringing your figure problems under control.

NCLINE SITUPS

The abdominal board should be at an angle of approximately 40 degrees. Beginners, however, should start with around 20 degrees. The head should be raised, the hands behind the neck. The upper body should then be raised and lowered repeatedly, breathing in as you rise and out as you go down.

HANGING LEG RAISES

This exercise is excellent for the lower area of the abdominal muscles. Lie on an abdominal board at an angle of between 20 and 30 degrees, bend the legs slightly and move them up and down. Do make sure that you maintain constant tension in the lower abdominal area. More advanced bodybuilders can also do this exercise on the bar dipper.

INCLINE LEG RAISES

In this exercise, the bent legs are raised without touching the body. Similarly on lowering they should not touch the floor, giving constant tension in the abdominal area. When bringing up the legs you should breathe in, and when lowering them you should breathe out.

MY TIP

Since you sweat a lot as you train, it is extremely important to drink mineral water even whilst you are training, to compensate for the loss of water.

WAIST TWIST

The hips may be classified a problem area as that is where any increase in weight first becomes visible. I recommend the following exercise. Position yourself on the front edge of a training bench, place a wooden bar at the neck, clasp it with the arms from behind and turn the upper body from left to right, facing forwards at all times. If you have a hip turner at the fitness centre (as shown in the illustrations), you can do the exercise even more efficiently.

MY TIP

Many people believe that at the end of his career and training, a bodybuilder's muscles hang in tatters. If a body has been trained every day for several hours, you cannot stop training overnight. In any high-performance sportsman this would be bound to lead to health problems.

It is important, therefore, to draw up a fitness programme that continues to keep the body in shape. You can, for example, gradually reduce the frequency and duration of training and change to 'normal food'. Running and cycling, swimming or gymnastics provide a good counterbalance for keeping the tissue firm in spite of a reduction in weight. This, of course, applies not only to bodybuilders but basically to all high-performance sportsmen.

DEVELOPING A TRAINING PROGRAMME

NUMBER OF SETS AND REPEATS

Every body responds differently to training. This is due less to physical make-up than to frame of mind and individual motivation. The number of sets and repeats is important. You should ensure that you always do seven correct repeats. Competitors should train beyond the pain threshold. Here, a partner can help with further repeats. It is only beyond this threshold that the muscle is stimulated, allowing it to grow and giving it the necessary division. Before going into threshold ranges it is extremely important to warm up with relatively light weights.

The number of repeats can quite easily be 15 or 20. These should be done in two sets to avoid serious injury.

A little tip from me: if you suffer any pain in the joints or tendons, immediately cool the affected area with ice, and for safety consult a doctor as soon as possible.

Initially, you must accustom yourself to the exercises slowly. Four sets of six to eight repeats each is a good number when beginning training. To begin with, three exercises per body part will be sufficient, ensuring that the three basic exercises, bench presses, squats and presses behind the neck are included.

Later, the number of exercises and sets can be increased. The number of repeats of the basic exercises should now be increased to eight. The number of repeats to build up muscle mass and strength should be between six and eight. If it is well over 12, the weight is too light. It must then be increased until six to eight repeats are reached again.

Only if you are training for a contest should you do another three or four above the recommended number of repeats: you could then vary the exercises, or do them with a partner. When varying them, however, you should be sure to do the exercise more or less correctly as it will not otherwise achieve the desired success and can even cause injury. Which explains my tip: never allow youself to be carried away by false pride, and don't use weights that are too heavy.

BEGINNERS

Number of training sessions: three times per week; training time: one hour per session.		
Exercises	Sets	Repeats
Monday: Calves, chest and abdomen		
Seated calf raises	4	8–10
Situps	3	6–8
Leg raises	3	6–8
Barbell presses on the Multipress	4	6–8
Dumbbell Flyes	4	6–8
Upright rowing	3	6–8
Tuesday: Calves, abdominals, back and arms		
Standing calf raises	4	8–10
Situps	3	6–8
Waist twists	–	5 mins.
Seated pulley rows – wide grip	3	8–10
Bent over laterals	3	8–10
Standing barbell curls	3	6–8
Standing triceps presses	3	6–8
Friday: Back, abdominals, shoulders and legs		
Hyper extensions	4	6–8
Hanging leg raises	4	6–8
Barbell presses on the shoulder machine	4	6–8
Upright rowing – cables	3	6–8
Leg extensions	4	6–8
Leg curls	4	6–8

CLOTHING AND SHOES

Since a bodybuilder does a wide range of exercises and so puts every fibre of his body under stress, he must of course wear the right clothes. They must take hard wear and must be easy to care for. The manufacturers have, of course, worked to these requirements. Very often the materials used are a cotton-viscose mix which quickly carries away the perspiration from the skin: i.e. the wearer does not feel cold so quickly, and remains comfortable over a relatively long period of training.

ADVANCED

Number of training sessions: four times per week; training time: one and a half hours per session.		
Exercises	Sets	Repeats
Monday: Calves, abdominals, chest and arms		
Seated calf raises	4	10–12
Situps	4	12–15
Free barbell bench presses	5	8–10
Dumbbell Flyes	4	8–10
Dumbbell pull-overs	4	8–10
Standing barbell curls	4	6–8
Standing triceps presses	4	6–8
Barbell or dumbbell curls on the Scott bench	4	6–8
Seated triceps dumbbell presses	4	6–8
Tuesday: Calves, abdominals, shoulders and back		
Leg raises	4	10–12
Presses behind the neck	4	8–10
Seated side lateral raises	4	6–8
Chins	4	6–8
Bent over rowing	4	6–8
T-bar rows	4	6–8
Two arm seated pulley rows	4	6–8
Thursday: Abdominals, legs, and calves		
Situps	5	10–12
Waist twists	–	5 mins.
Back squats	5	6–8
Incline leg presses	4	8–10
Lying leg biceps curls	5	8–10
Leg extensions	5	8–10
Standing calf raises	3	6–8
Seated calf raises	3	6–8
Friday: Back, chest and arms		
Deadlifts	4	6–8
Free dumbbell bench presses	4	8–10
Bench presses	4	6–8
Dumbbell pull-overs	3	8–10
Peck decks	3	6–8
Seated dumbbell curls	4	6–8
Narrow bench presses	4	6–8
Concentration curls	4	6–8
Bent over triceps exercise on the rope	4	6–8
Lower arm training on the bench	3	4–6

But often you can make do with the normal training suit available relatively cheaply in any department store or sports shop. For the reasons explained above, however, it is sensible to take a look at the material. Also make sure that the suit fits you well and gives sufficient freedom of movement. Otherwise, in the squat, for example you can suddenly find yourself exposed.

When you have developed a certain amount of muscle mass, you will find that your shirts, trousers or jackets constantly become too tight. You need to take this into account in your training wear, too. In sportswear, at least, the stores offer suits and sports shirts with a cut that allows for a broader back, and thicker upper arms and thighs.

True, as an active sportsman you also want to be fashionable. But there is a wide range of clothing available so that everyone can satisfy his own personal taste. For me, it is very important to wear clothing that motivates me, i.e. the muscles being trained must be visible. I want to be able to observe how the muscle works in training.

In many exercises, it is important to have a stable, non-slip stance. So you should always wear suitable footwear for training. For squats, for example, high sports shoes are recommended. Not only do these prevent sprains, they also provide a firmer stance. Otherwise a simple flat, air-permeable sports shoe will suffice.

A NUTRITION PROGRAMME

Nutrition plays quite an important part in bodybuilding. Sportsmen often think a lot about different training systems, training intensity, numbers of repeats and so on. Very often, however, the reason for stagnation in muscle building lies in the wrong diet.

They eat, for example, inferior foods such as white bread, cakes and biscuits made from bleached flour, and large quantities of chips, without reflecting whether or not this type of food is of any use to muscle building. 'Going for mass' does not mean that mass is the same as muscle. Of what use is a 44lb increase in weight in the form of fat, when you later have to lose between 37 and 39lbs for the muscles to be clearly visible.

It is much more sensible to design your diet to achieve continuous muscle growth with a relatively low body fat content. Together with effective training, this is best achieved by dividing the total calorie input for the day into four to five smaller meals per day. The advantage is obvious: with relatively small meals, the body is far better able to process the nutrients with which it is fed, rather than with three large meals which put the body under unnecessary stress.

You should avoid foods with a high proportion of refined sugar, white flour and fat. In a balanced diet for a sportsman, the energy should consist of approximately 60 per cent carbohydrate, 25 per cent protein and 15 per cent fat, and it should contain all the necessary vitamins and minerals. We obtain protein, for example, from lean meat, fish, dairy products and eggs. Carbohydrates are to be found in cereals, in fruit, vegetables, rice and potatoes. As the animal foodstuffs quoted already contain fat, only small quantities should be consumed in addition, in the form of a superior vegetable oil. Recommended drinks are skimmed milk, freshly squeezed fruit juices, tea, mineral water and coffee. The fibre contained in cereal products such as wholemeal bread, muesli, wholewheat pasta and brown rice, and in fruit and vegetables, is very important for the digestion.

In all foods, you should pay attention to freshness and careful preparation. I also recommend a nutritional supplement, taking sensible additives, as sportsmen have an increased requirement for protein, vitamins and minerals.

These include vitamin B complex, vitamins E and C and a mineral preparation. It is also beneficial to cover around 30 to 40 per cent of the protein requirement by a protein concentrate, as these contain no purine or other accompanying substances.

If you want to put on weight, you need to increase your calorie input. If you want to lose weight, reduce your calorie consump-

DIET PROGRAMMES

Weight increase: (Sportsman's weight: 176lb).				
1st meal	**Carbohydrate**	**Protein**	**Fat**	**cal**
5oz rolled oats	100	21	10	600
8oz cottage cheese	10	35	1	200
0.5l low-fat milk	24	16	8	250
1 slice wholemeal bread	21	4	1	110
2 spoonfuls honey	16	–	–	60
2nd meal	**Carbohydrate**	**Protein**	**Fat**	**cal**
10oz yoghurt	15	9	10	198
1 banana	30	1	–	135
2 oranges	28	–	–	160
3rd meal	**Carbohydrate**	**Protein**	**Fat**	**cal**
8oz rump steak	–	50	15	288
16oz potatoes	95	10	5	425
10oz brocccoli	12	9	–	100
1 portion mixed salad	25	6	–	150
4th meal	**Carbohydrate**	**Protein**	**Fat**	**cal**
2 slices wholemeal bread	42	8	2	220
4 spoonfuls honey	32	–	–	120
1 slice Edam	2	8	5	84
Protein drink with skimmed milk	10	48	10	420
5th meal	**Carbohydrate**	**Protein**	**Fat**	**cal**
8oz turkey breast	–	52	5	280
3oz rice	79	7	1	368
7oz pineapple	26	2	–	114
1 portion mixed salad	25	6	–	150
Total	612	292	73	4432

Weight loss: (Sportsman's weight: 176lb).				
1st meal	Carbohydrate	Protein	Fat	cal
8oz curd cheese	10	351	1	200
3oz rolled oats	66	14	7	402
1 slice wholemeal bread	21	4	1	110
2 spoonfuls honey	16	–	–	60
1 glass milk (0.2l)	10	6	3	90
2nd meal	Carbohydrate	Protein	Fat	cal
1 protein drink with skimmed milk	28	49	2	338
1 banana	30	–	–	135
3rd meal	Carbohydrate	Protein	Fat	cal
7oz turkey breast	–	42	4	220
3oz whole wheat pasta	72	14	1	390
1 portion mixed salad	40	10	–	230
4th meal	Carbohydrate	Protein	Fat	cal
10oz yoghurt	15	9	10	190
1½oz muesli	36	6	3	190
1 orange	14	–	–	80
5th meal	Carbohydrate	Protein	Fat	cal
7oz chicken	–	36	2	176
3oz rice	79	7	1	368
1 portion green salad	4	2	–	28
Total	441	204	35	3215

tion. In order not to put on superfluous fat, the calorie input should not be substantially higher than around 500 to 700 cal above our average requirement. To reduce body weight, the calorie balance should be undercut by 500 to 700 cals, as it is no longer possible to train effectively with a greater reduction in calorie consumption.

To determine the energy balance, you will require a nutritional values table and personal scales. The daily input of calories can then be calculated with the aid of the table, and the bodyweight checked. If your bodyweight remains constant, the quantity of calories consumed represents your personal energy balance.

It is important to consume carbohydrates approximately one to one and a half hours prior to training, and to eat protein directly after training, as the need is greatest at this point.

Whilst many fitness-seekers and sportsmen have found an excellent form of physical training in bodybuilding, the present-day stars of the sport, the contest athletes, often find themselves exposed to ridicule and criticism from large sectors of the population, as they generally exceed the limits of normal aesthetic appreciation through their muscle training.

Bodybuilding sports enthusiasts undoubtedly have the necessary sense of humour, even understanding, for this situation, since like so many things, aesthetic sense is ultimately a question of personal taste. The well-beloved weightlifter, footballers' legs, tennis players' arms or boxers' noses are gifts to the caricaturist. But it is incomprehensible that bodybuilding athletes who practise their sport seriously and have to work hard to win a contest, should be made fun of as 'brainless gorillas' and even denied recognition as sportsmen. Fortunately these are exceptions, and bodybuilding is well on the road to becoming a popular sport.

In West Germany, there are now some 5,000 bodybuilding and fitness training centres, with approximately four and a half million members. These include primarily the active bodybuilders, who have to be included in the performance sportsmen group on the basis of volume of training alone. They train four to five times per week, for two to three hours at a time, and most take part in regional or supra-regional contests and championships.

A further very large group estimated at five million and attending fitness training centres on a sporadic basis only take their personal programme no less seriously. In most cases their main concern is to achieve general physical fitness, to maintain or attain their ideal weight and a generally attractive figure.

Bodybuilding is an ideal method of specifically training particular parts of the body. Women are well represented in both interest groups. In addition there is also a large circle of people who make use of the therapeutic orthopaedic effects of certain bodybuilding exercises and go for training once or twice a week as treatment.

The training machines in the fitness centres can also be used for sport for the handicapped. Certain muscle groups that need to be particularly strong because of a physical handicap can be strengthened by the right exercises. Not only does this training help the handicapped to greater achievement, it also provides an attractive leisure sport that brings handicapped and non-handicapped together. Finally, given the low risk of injury, bodybuilding is also suitable for the elderly, helping them to maintain their own optimum physical condition. The older we get, the more important it is to do something to keep us in trim.

All in all, bodybuilding has been gaining in significance at international level. This is evident not least in the existence of three bodybuilding associations, of which one has acquired worldwide recognition with 132 national member associations. It is in turn a member of the International Federation of Sports Associations and of the 'World Games'. The German section of this association is the IFBB-Germany, a union of fitness training centre operators in that country.

The German 'Verband der Bodybuilder' (Association of Bodybuilders) has now developed to become the world's leading association, ahead of the United States, this being illustrated in particular by the world championship titles won in 1985 and 1986 by both men and women.

The significance of bodybuilding is also evident in the number of specialist magazines available, the most important being 'Sportrevue', 'Sport & Fitness' and 'Flex'. The situation internationally is similar, as every member country of the IFBB also has its own magazines, some of which are published under licence from major American magazines.

STARTING OUT

Only a few athletes make the headlines in bodybuilding and only around one per cent of all those who practise bodybuilding do so to participate in contests. The remaining 99 per cent come to the training centres for quite different reasons. With the aid of the highly effective exercises on the equipment, they aim to keep fit, improve their figures or strengthen and tighten groups of muscles that are neglected in everyday life.

The fact that these objectives can be achieved by a reasonable bodybuilding training programme has been proved beyond doubt. Not only does it improve appearance; it also makes the subject stronger and more resistant and strengthens the heart and circulation. Regularly overcoming the baser instincts in training makes it easier to cope with difficult day-to-day problems and not to give in. It is important, however, to have the proper, specialist instruction when training. The beginner will initially feel bewildered by the range of facilities available in a fitness training centre.

Any newcomer should seek advice and assistance from a qualified instructor. Before an instructor puts together an individual programme, he finds out what the individual wants to achieve through his training. To be able to give proper training advice, the instructor needs to discuss the individual's health, fitness, physical strengths and weaknesses. In this way, every part of the body can be trained appropriately: i.e. more intensive attention can be paid during exercises to weak muscles that are put under less stress.

The instructor ensures that the training programme is not one-sided, that the exercises are done correctly, and that the correct weights are applied.

Anyone from the age of 15 to 70 can practise bodybuilding. It is particularly important for the young to follow a tailormade training programme, as the body is still growing. Never work with weights that are too heavy.

Even if you have never played any sport before, you can go into fitness training at any time. Don't feel shy about going to a fitness training centre. You will meet many like-minded and like-built people who wont necessarily be training towards a Mr. Universe title. You will receive a friendly welcome even from the high performance athletes, because your desire to do something for your body will meet with a warm reception among the bodybuilding and fitness training community.

STAGES OF LIFE

THE PRIVATE MAN

Ralf Möller was born in Recklinghausen on 12 January 1959. At 23in, he won his first championship straight away, as the largest baby in the ward. His parents, Ursula and Helmut, were naturally proud of their eight and a half pound son, who was to be their only child.

Ralf first took an active part in sports at the age of seven: he joined the Recklinghaus SV Neptune swimming club. His sponsor from those days, Ortwin Thum, one of the founders of the swimming club, is still one of his closest friends. Until the age of 15, Ralf remained loyal to the sport of swimming. For six years, he practised competitive swimming and even won a number of town and Westphalian championships. He then trained for two years at the 'Boxring 28' boxing club in Recklinghausen although he never fought.

At the end of a two and a half year commercial college training, he began a further two and a half year's training as a swimming instructor for the Recklinghausen local authority. In 1983 he requested leave from this activity. The understanding is that he may return to his old job at any time. He was supported by the office manager, the municipal director and even the mayor.

In the meantime, his mother, Ursula, had become a real specialist in the field of sportsmen's nutrition, as for many years she had been putting together the right nutritional programme for Ralf, cooking it all herself of course. Father, Helmut, handles the daily mail. From him, his son inherited single-mindedness, and it is this characteristic that has ultimately brought Ralf to where he is today. His father also, of

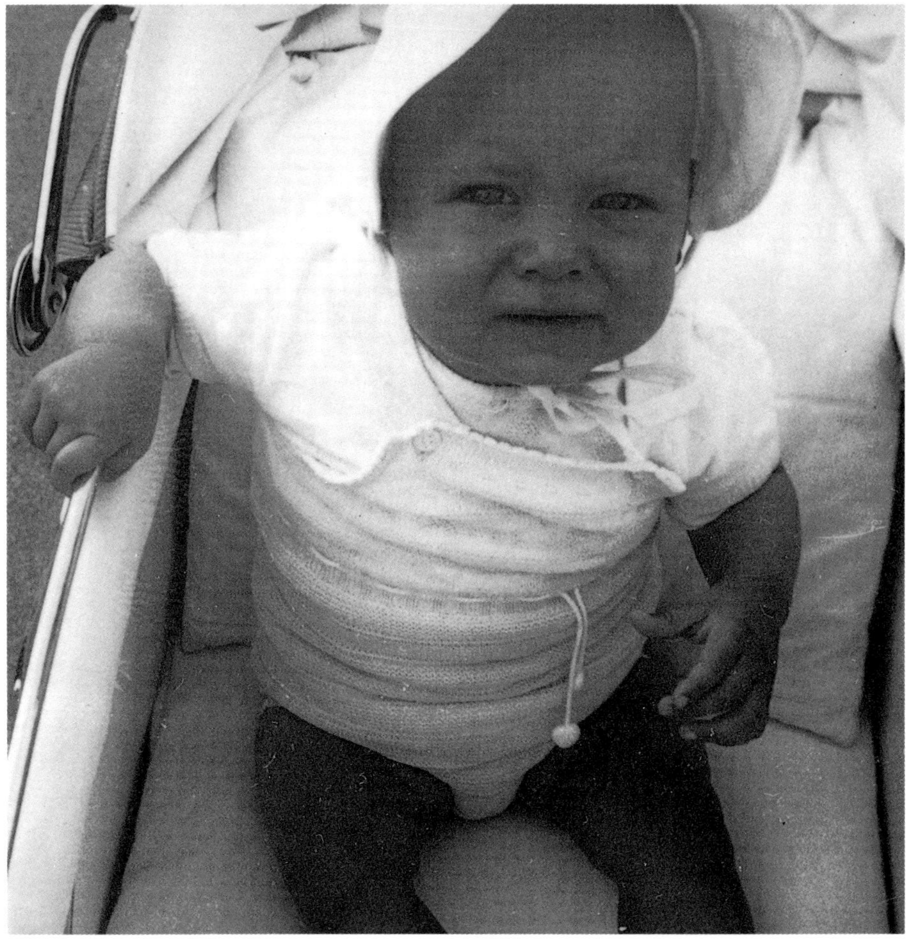

At the age of seven months (top), Ralf Möller as yet shows no muscles. But by the age of seven (left) he is already 'posing' and enjoying the fresh air of the Bavarian woods with his father (above).

Page 99: Ralf Möller with his parents . . . with his car . . . and in Hawaii.

course, occasionally watches his training.

In addition to his passion for bodybuilding, now his occupation, there are, of course, other things in Ralf Möller's life. His love of painting, for example. He owns some water colours by Kohler and a number of oil paintings by Hettingen – two German painters whose work relates solely to modern sports themes.

As well as modern art, he also likes modern, tasteful décors. This is clear in the flat which he owns near the Recklinghausen municipal park and which he has furnished himself.

Music, too, is one of his hobbies. Grace Jones, Tina Turner, Al Jarreau and Stevie Wonder, all representatives of 'black' music, are among his favourite artists. Ralf has also developed a liking for the German, Peter Hofmann, possibly because this successful singer, a former decathlete, practises a lot of sport himself to keep fit.

And Ralf's other interests? They include reading, good food, good films with such actors as Jack Nicholson, Dustin Hoffman or Robert de Niro, diving, and a weakness for fast cars. Having previously had a 3.2 litre Porsche Carrera Cabriolet, he currently drives a Mercedes 500 SEC, a luxury that his successful sporting career, together with its various business 'sidelines', has allowed him. He has already travelled virtually the entire world: Yugoslavia, England, Austria, Switzerland, Spain, Holland, Sweden, Belgium, and also the United States, Africa, Singapore, Sri Lanka, Japan and Hawaii. But Ralf Möller is not merely a bon viveur: he has to work very hard for his success.

And there is another Ralf Möller too: one who helps raise money in campaigns for sufferers from multiple sclerosis, or supports and promotes Greenpeace campaigns . . .

Ralf Möller enjoys the beautiful panorama of Honolulu (above) from a helicopter. Even here, it is carrying him to a fitness training centre (with an acquaintance, Cory Eversen, and his fiancée Annette).

At the end of January 1987, Ralf Möller visited Senegal and its capital city Dakar, accompanied by his mother and Annette.

HIS CAREER

A Capricorn never gives up. Above all others, this statement typifies the career of Ralf Möller, who came across a true bodybuilder for the first time in Yugoslavia in 1976. The 17-year-old Ralf Möller had travelled there on holiday with his parents.

'My attention was drawn to this man, because he looked different from all the others with his muscles,' recounts Ralf Möller. This was his first contact in the flesh with a bodybuilder, an athlete he had previously only ever come across in magazines. 'I soon got talking to him, as he came from a neighbouring city – more precisely from Essen. We talked about his training, and I discovered that he trained for one to two hours, three to four times a week.'

As a 17 year old (above) Ralf was at the start of his bodybuilding career. The photograph (right) shows him as an 18 year old. The 'Professional' (top right) looks quite different, with (left to right) Albert Beckels, Lee Haney and Walter Herden and in 1986 with Jürgen Brand (p. 103).

There can be no doubt that it is largely a question of the targets that you set yourself. If you want to take part in contests (and, where possible, to win them too) you can't get around the need to train for two to three hours up to six times a week. But Ralf Möller was a long way from that at this stage.

On his return home, he lost none of his initial enthusiam for bodybuilding. His father welded him two dumbbells. 'I spent a lot of time with them in the cellar, and I still remember today that I did thirty or forty repeats of exercises that I had dreamt up myself and that couldn't in fact produce any muscle growth. But of course, I didn't know that at the time.'

At the end of his secondary education, Ralf Möller attended a commercial college. As his activities as a swimmer then came to an end, Ralf considered how he could keep himself sporting fit. His first port of call was a boxing club, where he trained twice weekly. There he met Manfred Pospich, an active bodybuilder.

'At that time, in 1977, there were very few fitness training centres as we know them today. They certainly weren't as widespread. I went to Herne with Manfred, to a room that was rather like a studio, and initially I was happy to have exercise apparatus available to me to train the individual muscle groups specifically. But the room was anything but attractive, although that did nothing to dampen my initial enthusiasm. The dumbbells and apparatus were rusty, and in winter you had to wear a pullover as there were draughts from every nook and cranny. There were, of course, no showers.'

But for Ralf, all that counted was the training. He went to Herne twice or three times a week. As he did not at that stage have a car of his own, he had to do the journey by public transport. Life was by no means as convenient as it is today for bodybuilding enthusiasts, with fitness training centres virtually at every turn.

It might be worth quoting a few statistics here: Munich has around 100 centres, Cologn 70 to 80, and even Ralf Möller's home town, Recklinghausen, has seven in the town centre and many others in the immediate environs. At the end of the seventies, as stated, it took a great deal more energy and time to get to the 'much sought after iron'.

'But it was quite good, because it made you want to train all the more! In my first fitness centre, I naturally met lots of like-minded people, some of whom were very single-minded in their muscle building. Some of it must have rubbed off onto me. I still remember that my dream weight for the bench press was 198lb. I greatly admired a bodybuilder who was able to push this weight seven or eight times in succession. It was Manfred Pospich, who had introduced me to the studio.'

It was still some time before this first 198lb target was reached, as at the age of 17½, Ralf Möller began with weights of 77 and 88lb. A few months later, Ralf acquired his own key and was then able to arrange his training as he wished. Through a friend, he shortly afterwards entered the bodybuilding scene in Essen.

'I met Walter Herden, who practised bodybuilding himself but had no competitive ambitions. His interest was generally keeping fit. His main occupation was as caretaker of a school, and he also built fitness apparatus. Back in 1977, he would certainly never have dreamed that it might lead to the famous firm of Gym 80 which he runs with his partner, Peter Förster. And I would never have believed that I would

1982 World Championship in Bruges: Gunnar Rosbo, winner Lee Haney, and Ralf Möller.

Ralf Möller in 1978 with Walter Herden at the Brand Studio.

one day make a living from bodybuilding.'

Through Walter Herden, Ralf met his subsequent friend and training partner Jürgen Brand, whom he already knew from magazines as an active and, most importantly, successful bodybuilder. In 1972, Jürgen Brand was already German Junior Champion. Even among the seniors, he was very successful, and was to remain so in subsequent years. In 1982, Brand took first place in the German IFBB championships in the under 198lb class. He had opened his own studio just a few weeks before.

Jürgen Brand watched Ralf in training, saw the level of performance that he had already

achieved through his work in Herne, and asked him whether he would be interested in competing. He was to compete in February 1978 in the Saalbau, Essen, for the Junior Championship. Ralf Möller had given no thought to competing at that stage, as he was primarily interested only in physical fitness and an athletic appearance. He had, however, already started posing.

The 1978 championship was Ralf's first public appearance, which he completed successfully, taking third place. He was naturally spurred on by this success, and the public doubtless wondered where this giant had come from: at the height of 6 ft 4 inches, even today he is unquestionably a unique figure in bodybuilding.

One week later he had a telephone call from Albert Busek, current President of the IFBB, who had acted as agent for Arnold Schwarzenegger when he went to America back in 1968. Ralf recalls: 'Albert invited me to Munich where he and his family extended great hospitality to me. He asked me whether I was really serious about bodybuilding. Following my success in Essen, I was bound to answer yes. A few weeks later, I took part in a Bavarian championship at Landshut, which I won.

'In one conversation, Albert pointed out to me that bodybuilding was also a matter of proportions and for this reason an athlete of my size would find it particularly difficult. At the same time, however, he encouraged me to carry on. This conversation dispelled my final doubts and after my two championship successes, I really set to work for the first time.

'In the same year, 1978, I took part in the IFBB German Championship and was winner of my class at the first attempt. In the final contest for the overall championship, I had to compete against a smaller athlete, Gabriel Wild, who at a height of 5 ft 7 inches was not only better proportioned than I was, but also an excellent poser. I sensed for myself there that my physical size,

which I had initially considered an advantage, was more of a handicap.

'I would have needed at least 22lb more muscle mass to beat this athlete.

'Naturally I continued training, as my target was to be overall winner among the juniors. Every day, in my first car, given to my by my father, I drove from Recklinghausen to Essen. Not only did Jürgen himself train in the Brand Studio, but also other bodybuilders, such as Hans Baus, who was highly successful at the end of the seventies. Naturally the conditions are very much more favourable if a number of contest-oriented athletes train together, as the vast majority of those who train are only fitness-oriented.'

In 1979, Ralf Möller mounted a new attack on overall victory, but once again he 'only' managed to win his class. At that time, the 19 year old weighed around 253lb. The overall winner was Karl Link, an athlete of around 5 ft 7 inches. At the time, Ralf had already been in the Federal Armed Forces for six weeks. Basic training naturally made it difficult to prepare for further contests. Thanks to Albert Busek, who wrote to the Armed Forces, Ralf was able to continue his training without interruption right up to the contest.

'The people there showed a lot of understanding for my sport. I was often allowed to leave early in order to get to training on time.'

But Ralf never forgot to visit his parents. His mother always knew how to prepare the right food for a bodybuilder, though Ralf did not yet properly understand it.

'For me, the main thing was the training, and I didn't pay much attention to the right food.'

In view of his size, Ralf should, even then, have been eating between 8oz and 16oz of protein with a probable calorie requirement of 4000 to 5000. Today, the figures are rather different: calorie requirement, 6000 to

1982 **World Championship in Bruges. Comparative posing with Gunnar Rosbo (above) and at the winner's ceremony with Lee Haney (p. 107).**

8000, protein requirement between 12 and 14oz. But Ralf knew nothing of that at the time. So – like many others – he lacked the necessary consistency of diet and the awareness that training alone does not guarantee victory in contests.

'60 per cent training and 40 per cent nutrition is the right balance. If a salesman only withdraws money from the till, he will very soon be broke! It's exactly the same with our bodies. Today, I eat something every three to four hours throughout the day. In that way I can maintain my weight, and I still have reserves for increasing it for contests.'

However, during his Federal Armed Forces period, Ralf Möller no longer trained so regularly, as he was suffering a certain sense of frustration at his failure to win overall. He trained in the shot put, but mainly stayed in the dumbbell room. But immediately after the Armed Forces, he began training intensively again in bodybuilding.

In 1982, for the first time, Ralf Möller became German number two in the 'Big Class'; the class and overall winner at that time was Wilhelm Hauck. In spite of this, it was a giant start among the seniors. In the autumn of the same year, the world championships took place in Bruges, Belgium. Ralf had set himself the target of coming among the first six. That he finally took third place was a huge surprise. In the space of only a year he had succeeded in catapulting himself to the amateur world peak.

The winner was Lee Haney, extremely well-known to insiders, and who to date has already won the 'Mr. Olympia' title three times. Second place went to twice runner-up Gunnar Rosbo. 'Gunnar was only one point ahead of me,' says Ralf, to show how near he was to coming second, and how highly valued his third place should be.

In 1983, he went to Singapore. 'Of course I wanted to win and become overall winner.' Ralf was up against two exceptional athletes, Bob Paris and Berry de Mey. 'Both were around 5 ft 9 inches tall and beat me because of their better proportions. True I weighed 269lb at the time, but it was still too little. It was of no use to me to be the best defined: I still lacked muscle mass and physical harmony.'

Prior to this world championship in May, Ralf Möller had become German champion in Munich. It was a particularly important success, as he became overall winner of all classes in this contest.

'In 1984 in Las Vegas, I wanted finally to come first. So I paid more attention than previously to the right food. I had to eat several times a day to achieve my protein quota of 12 to 14oz and to take in the necessary quantity of carbohydrate.'

At that time, Ralf Möller was still working as a swimming instructor for the Recklinghausen local authority. It was not until 1984 that he resigned to prepare properly for the world championships in Las Vegas. This, of course, meant that he had no salary. He was training morning and afternoon. Given the interest in Germany and Europe, however, he managed to bring in the 'necessary wherewithal' through seminars and guest appearances. However, in 1984 Ralf was so busy travelling and attending seminars that he was unable to train properly. Hence his participation in the world championship was postponed until 1985.

1984 was also a very significant time for Ralf Möller in another respect. He met the girl who is now his fiancée, Annette. Her initial impressions of bodybuilding are best explained in her own words.

Training in Singapore.

'To be perfectly honest, initially I thought bodybuilding was quite gruesome. I was frightened by all those muscles. But when I got to know Ralf better, his ways and character, I saw in him only a lovable, understanding partner, and resigned myself to his passion for bodybuilding. Only later when I began training myself and felt how much good this sport was doing me did my interest begin to grow – doubtless as a result of Ralf's influence, too. And today I can get quite enthusiastic about bodybuilding and a well-trained muscular body.'

'First she watched. In 1985 she began training herself.' Ralf says with great pride. 'Now she trains four times a week, in each case

At the weight check for the 1983 World Championship in Singapore, Ralf Möller (left) was still full of hopes that he would succeed. Top: First round of the contests in Singapore.

for an hour. Not, of course, to take part in contests, but for fun and fitness.'

Annette is 5 ft 5 inches tall and weighs 114lb. That isn't the only reason why she is a good foil to Ralf. She isn't the kind to agree with everything: she always has her own opinion.

'Since Annette goes to work during the day, we are occasionally able to train together in the centre which is run superbly by Monica Herden and where I have been training since 1984.'

In Singapore, Ralf Möller measured himself against Lee Haney and Gunnar Rosbo (above). Bottom left – 'Ripped and Rugged!' Bottom right – 'Beefy, most muscular!'

Page 111: The bodybuilder's chest.

In 1985, bodybuilding developed into a business for Ralf Möller, too. In addition to the numerous seminars which were becoming ever more popular, the first major companies also came to Ralf Möller with advertising contracts. Not only, therefore, did he have to carry out his stringent training, he also had to ensure that his business contracts were properly negotiated and fulfilled.

'Over this period, I met the man who is now my adviser and friend, Klaus Linke, who runs a tax consultancy office with his brother in Gelsenkirchen. It was with Klaus that I negotiated the first important contracts, and I am certain that there is still a lot of interesting work awaiting us. Together with my solicitor, Schmitz, who handles the legal problems, we make up a good team. I am very glad, as it would be too much for me to handle all these various time-consuming affairs.'

1985 was to be Ralf Möller's year – or so at least he thought. He was resolutely pursuing his objective of finally becoming world champion, and launched a further attack on the IFBB (International Federation of Bodybuilding) heavyweight world championship title.

The IFBB contest judges have to undergo an intensive training program in their individual national associations. Each year, in addition, they are tested on the knowledge and abilities that they have acquired. Erich Janner, Managing Director of the IFBB and an international contest judge for years, has so far remained infallible, thus earning himself the nickname among his friends of 'Mr. 100 per cent'. In contests where measurements and stopwatch are absent, a cer-

The illustrations on this page show Ralf Möller's hard training during preparations for the 1986 Tokyo World Championship.

tain personal sympathy quite naturally always influences decisions.

Ice skaters and gymnasts too, for example, have to reconcile themselves to this fact.

'Everything went very well. Four weeks prior to the contest, I weighed 295lb', says Ralf. 'True I still lacked hardness in the legs, but I still had sufficient time to train'. And then it happened. The nightmare and disappointment. Ralf suffered a serious injury to his shoulder joint. Normally stoppage of three weeks would have been necessary, but that would have meant that the world championships were out. Several times a week, Ralf was given injections by Dr. Rabl Toma, the weightlifters' association doctor. The treatment certainly lessened the pain, but could not eliminate it entirely.

By the time of the contest in Gothenborg, Ralf had lost almost 22lb. As a result, his hopes of having the right proportions in spite of his enormous body size were dashed. Ralf Möller came only fifth.

'I had one or two days to think about it, then I was all right again. I want finally to prove that even a big athlete could win the title. I was the largest, or rather I wasn't yet at that time: I was merely the tallest and heaviest bodybuilder in the world. But I wanted the world championship title – in part, too, to show to all contestants over 6 ft 2 inches that they could do it.'

In 1986 he finally succeeded. This really was Ralf Möller's year, although in qualification in Augsburg two weeks before the world championship he still almost failed, because – as in previous years – he still lacked the necessary definition on stage. But if he had reached top form too soon, he would probably have been unable to hold on to it until the world championship.

'For me, it was a matter of

ORLD
BUILDING
SHIPS
N 1986
105

precise timing. I had to be sure to keep my muscle mass to be able to appear at 280lb in good proportion and well defined on the day of the world championship. For that, I owed a great deal to my mother, who had been concerned with my contest diet for years.

'Together with my training partner Jürgen Konrade, who had already taken excellent care of me in 1985, and Ralf Röhr, a long-standing acquaintance from Recklinghausen, I prepared for the '86 world champtionship. Walter Klock, Helmet Wagner, Erich Janner and Prof. Dr. Beuker, IFBB association doctor since 1985, took care of the national team, of myself, Hermann Hoffend, Erwin Knoller and Karl-Heinz Loose.'

In Tokyo, success was finally on Ralf's side. He achieved his objective. He became world champion (and his team came second). It was a title that had a particular quality in 1986 as dope tests were carried out for the first time in the history of bodybuilding at a world championship. These tests being a prerequisite for recognition at the Olympic Games. The checks were carried out by none other than the celebrated Prof. Dr. Konicke from Cologne who, together with one American and one Japanese colleague, ensured that everything was done legally.

'With my size, I weighed 280lb. No one had done that before. And it was done for the first time for the world championship title recognized by the IOC.' Now Ralf Möller really was the 'biggest' in the truest sense of the word.

Following the world championship title, the next objective for Ralf Möller had to be the 'Mr. Olympia' title. 'This title was created by Joe Weider to give contestants who already have a world championship title an incentive to train for a further title.'

But sporting objectives are not the only ones of significance for Ralf. He knows how quickly a sporting career can come to an end – through a serious injury, for example. One venture to make life secure could be the founding of his own fitness centre and body building studio in his home town of Recklinghausen.

The interests of fitness enthusiasts are very close to his heart, but since Ralf would certainly not be able to be at the studio every day as a result of his other activities, he would work together with a number of qualified trainers who would run the training in line with his ideas.

Finally made it: the winner's ceremony in Tokyo with Ben Weider (p. 114).

Below: The world champion with his fiancée, Annette.

'Bodybuilding and fitness training only make sense if they are carried out with suitable equipment under sensible guidance,' says Ralf, and we know how right he is.

When a bodybuilding athlete with the physical dimensions and muscle mass of a Ralf Möller is so successful, it isn't long before the film producers are there. But not every offer is as interesting as it may appear at the outset. Some of the scriptwriters have still not shaken off the idea of the muscle-packed illiterate, whilst others see only a symbol of brutality in the bodybuilder.

But Ralf detests films that glorify violence. 'There shouldn't be hundreds of litres of blood being spilled. There are other dramatic means of creating tension!' Film producers such as Arthur Brauner or Horst Wendland appear to share this opinion, as they are already in negotiation with Ralf.

Ralf Möller, businessman, in discussion with adviser Klaus Linke and lawyer Herbert Schmitz (top). The world champion is also eager to nurture the younger generation (left, with Jürgen Konrade and young Lesley Herden).

World class athletes posing in the studio: Norbert Albrecht, Jusup Wilcosz, Ralf Möller, Peter Hensel and Thomas Scheu (p.117 top). Ralf Möller often used to train at the Busek-Sportcenter in Munich (p. 117 bottom).

BUSEK
Sport
CENTER
OLYMP
GYM

BUSEK
Sport
CENTER

HISTORY AND THEORY

ORIGIN AND MEANING

The sculpture of the ancient world had as an ideal of beauty a well-formed, muscular body. The models for many sculptors from the time of classical Greece were well trained athletes. The work and studies of Leonardo de Vinci and his students on the anatomy of the human body also give an indication of the ideal beauty of a later period, the Renaissance, influenced by the ancient world. Like Michelangelo they had a predilection for athletic models.

For a long time, the ideal of the muscular, strong and healthy body was then forgotten. It was not until the second half of the 19th century that it was revived. Strength and muscles, however, were not regarded as prerequisites for boxing and ring sports, but as an objective in themselves, a glorification of the harmoniously developed body.

Among the first men who attracted public admiration and even demonstrated strength exercises were Eugene Sandow, George Hackenschmidt, Hermann Goerner and many others. Like many initially eccentric-seeming sports, bodybuilding too was practised enthusiastically in the USA. There, in 1904, something like the first contest was held, the 'best built man in the USA.' (Mister USA) being chosen.

In the thirties, true bodybuilding began to develop, with dumbbell and machine training and gymnastic exercises. In 1940, the first real contest was held in America. Organizations were founded, and in the seventies the International Federation of Bodybuilders, today one of the largest sports associations in the world, was created.

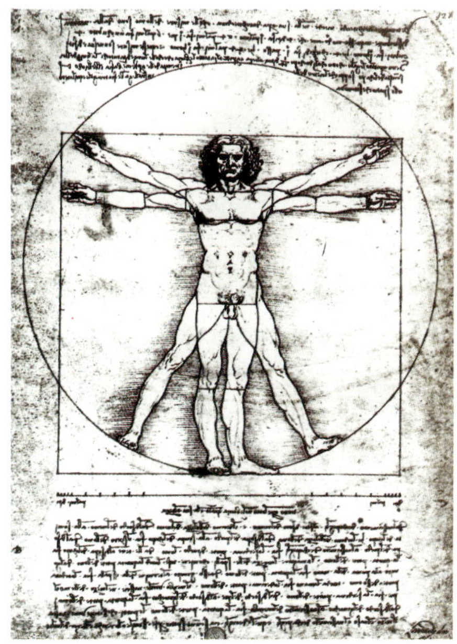

Even in days gone by, people had a predilection for athletic bodies.

P. 120: The Farnese Hercules by Glycon (1 century B.C.).
Top left: The bound slave of Michelangelo (1475–1564).
Top right: Hercules, an antique marble statue (sculptor unknown).
Centre right: Proportion drawing by Leonardo da Vinci (1452–1519).
Bottom left: Advertising poster for an athlete (Colour lithograph, 1899).

BODYBUILDING POSES

B.B.
PRO
SINGAPORE

THE SIGNIFICANCE AND ROLE OF POSING

Although you might perhaps believe that posing is only of significance for competitors, it can be of benefit even to the beginner, as it improves muscle structure and hardness. Posing is always, therefore, a good end to a training session, and is also useful for checking your achievement so far.

In a contest, the compulsory poses play a particular role as they have to be performed precisely as stipulated. In all, the competitor has seven compulsory poses: double biceps front, latissimus front, side chest pose, double biceps from the rear, the side triceps pose and the abdomen and leg pose, in which the arms have to be placed behind the head.

In each pose, muscle groups should be tensed and the individual poses must correspond exactly to the specifications given by the association – in the form of photographs. Judging involves a wide variety of criteria, for example muscle mass, muscle division, proportion, muscularity, definition. Accuracy of execution and the athlete's personality are also of significance to the judges.

In addition to the compulsory part, the contestant has 60 seconds available for freestyle, which he can individually design with music and his own poses. Here, the judges assess design creativity, transitions into the individual poses, sequence of movements, facial expression (no grimaces as a result of straining), and overall impression, taking into account the most widely varying criteria, such as harmony, muscle mass, proportions etc..

I.F. B.B

I.F. B.B.
136